First Words Writing and Comprehension

Introduction

Phase 2 of 'Letters and Sounds', (Crown copyright 2007), introduces 19 letters of the alphabet to be taught at the rate of four letters a week. These are:

s, a, t, p, i, n, m, d, g, o, c, k (k), e, u, r, h, b, f, l.

These activity sheets provide writing practice for these letters in simple CVC words.
The words 'I' and 'the' are introduced.
The connecting words 'on, off, in, and' are used in phrases, and the verbs 'can, am' are used in sentences beginning with 'I'.
'I' is the only capital letter used.

Handwriting the letters

The letters in this book have all been printed using the Sassoon Infant typeface. This font aims to teach children the hand movements associated with writing each letter of the alphabet.

The letters are grouped together in the same way as the DfEE publications 'Developing Early Writing' (2001), and 'Letters and Sounds' (2007).

c a d o g q e involve an anticlockwise movement of the hand.
m n h b p r k begin with a downward movement of the hand which is then retraced upward and followed by a clockwise movement.
t l u i j y begin with a downward movement of the hand followed by a turn at the bottom of the stroke.
s f ... have an anticlockwise movement followed by a clockwise movement.
v w x z k ... use straight lines only.
The letters q j y v w x z are not introduced in Phase 2, and hence are not used in this workbook.

Marlene Greenwood   July 2010

Writing Activities for First Words Series

Contents

1. Contents
2. Write *c, o.*
3. Write *a,* then *c, a, o.*
4. Write *t,* then *c, o, a, t.*
5. Write *r,* then *rat.*
6. Write *h,* then *hat.*
7. Write over dotted *cat, hat, rat, cot, hot.*
8. Draw lines to *a cat, a hat, a rat a cot*
9. Write *s,* then *cats.*
10. Write *e,* then *e, o, c, a, s.*
11. Write *n,* then *n, h, r.*
12. Draw lines to *ten, hen, net.*
13. Write *g,* then *g, a, o, e.*
14. Write *d,* then *d, o, a, c, g.*
15. Write over dotted *egg, eggs, dog, dogs.*
16. Write *b,* then *bat, bed.*
17. Write over dotted *bag, bad, bat, bed.*
18. Write *a* in *cat, hat, sad, bag, bad, bat, rat.*
19. Write *e* in *net, ten, hen, bed, den.*
20. Write *i,* then *in a bin.*
21. Write *f,* then *on, off.*
22. Write *l,* then *l, i, f, t.*
23. Draw lines to *log, fat, fan, lid.*
24. Write *o* in *dog, cot, hot, log, on, off.*
25. Write *m* then *m, n, h, r.*
26. Write *u* then *bus, sun.*
27. Write over dotted *hug, sun, bun, bud.*
28. Write *p* then *pin, pen.*
29. Write *i* in *bin, tin, pin, lip, lid.*
30. Write *u* in *hut, sun, bus, bun, bud.*
31. Write *k* then *kitten.*
32. Write *k* then *kitten.*
33. Write over phrases with adjectives.
34. Write over dotted words *the.*
35. Write over dotted phrases *on.*
36. Draw lines to phrases starting with *on.*
37. Write over dotted phrases *in.*
38. Draw lines to phrases starting with *in.*
39. Write over dotted *and.*
40. Draw lines to phrases containing *and.*
41. Write over dotted *I am ....*
42. Write over dotted *I can ....*
43. Draw lines to sentences with *I am.*
44. Draw lines to sentences with *I can.*
45. Mixed *I am in* and *I am on.*
46. Match words to pictures.

Activities from Jelly and Bean

Name.............................. Date........................

Write over the dotted letters. Then write the letters by yourself.

c c c c
c c c c
c c c c

....

o o o o
o o o o
o o o o

....

Activities from Jelly and Bean

2

Name.............................. Date..............................

Write over the dotted letters. Then write the letters by yourself.

....

....

Activities from Jelly and Bean

Name.......................... Date..........................
Write over the dotted letters. Then write the letters by yourself.

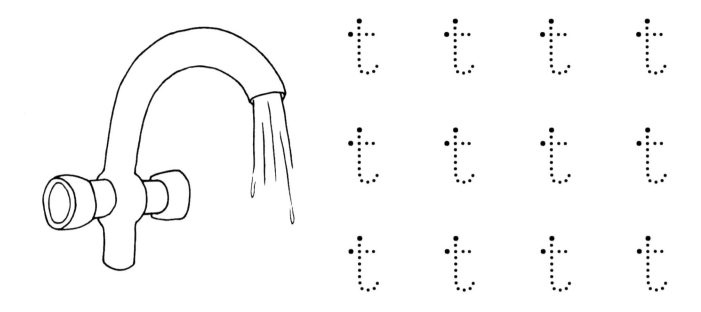

....

c o a t c a

o c t o c a

t a o t c t

....
Activities from Jelly and Bean

Name.............................. Date..............................

Write over the dotted letters. Then write the letter by yourself.

....

Write the over the dotted words. Then write the words by yourself.

....

Activities from Jelly and Bean

Name.............................. Date..............................

Write over the dotted letters. Then write the letter by yourself.

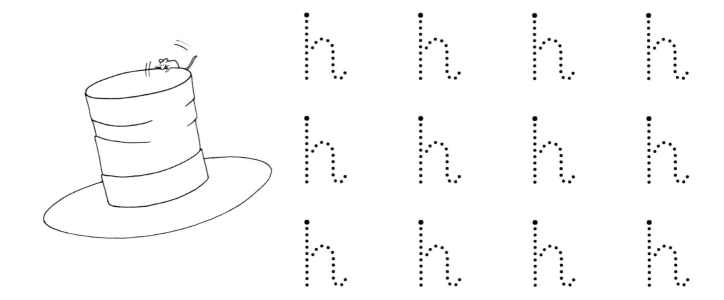

....

Write the over the dotted words. Then write the words by yourself.

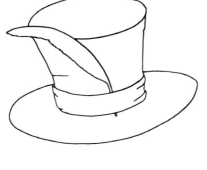

....

Activities from Jelly and Bean

Name.......................... Date..........................

Write over the dotted words.

| cat cot rat hat hot |

Say each word to a friend.

Activities from Jelly and Bean

Name.......................... Date...........................

Draw a line from the words to the correct picture.

Write the words.

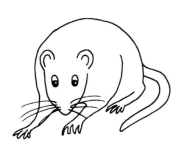

| a hat | a cat |
| a cot | a rat |

....

....

....

....

Activities from Jelly and Bean

Name.............................. Date..............................

Write over the dotted letters. Then write the letter by yourself.

....

Write the over the dotted words. Then write the words by yourself.

....

Activities from Jelly and Bean

Name............................... Date...........................

Write over the dotted letters. Then write the letters by yourself.

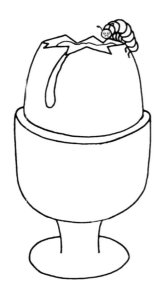

e e e e
e e e e
e e e e

....

e c o a e o
c a e c o a

....

....

Activities from Jelly and Bean

10

Name............................ Date............................

Write over the dotted letters. Then write the letters by yourself.

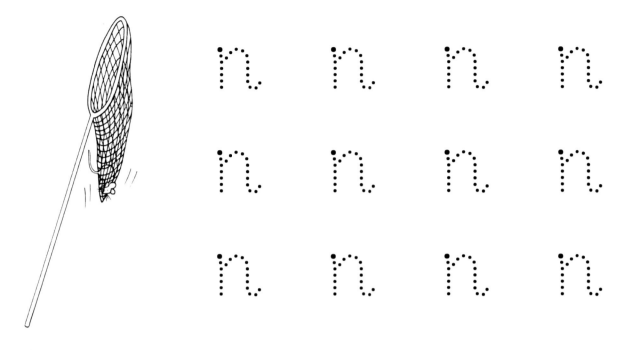

n n n n
n n n n
n n n n

....

n r h n r h
r n h r h n
n h r h n r

....

Activities from Jelly and Bean

Name.............................. Date..............................

Draw a line from each word to the correct picture.

Write the correct word next to each picture.

| net | ten | hen |

....

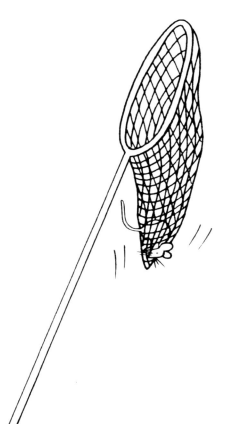

....

....

Name.............................. Date............................

Write over the dotted letters. Then write the letters by yourself.

....

g a g a g a
e g g e g g
g o g o g o

....

Activities from Jelly and Bean

Name.......................... Date..........................

Write over the dotted letters. Then write the letters by yourself.

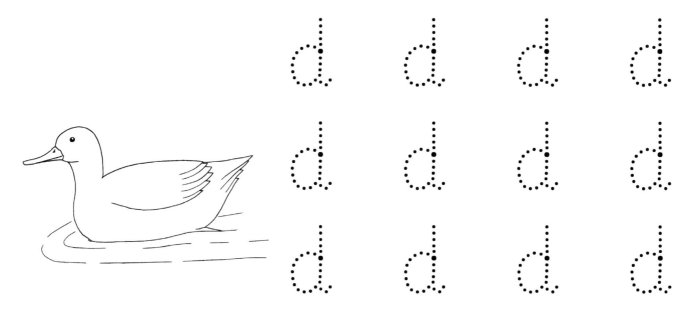

Activities from Jelly and Bean

Name.......................... Date..........................

Write the over the dotted words. Then write the words by yourself.

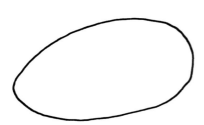 

....

Write the over the dotted words. Then write the words by yourself.

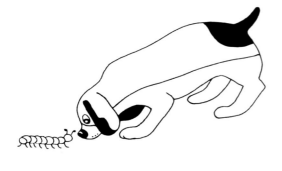  

....

Activities from Jelly and Bean

Name.............................. Date..............................

Write over the dotted letters. Then write the letter by yourself.

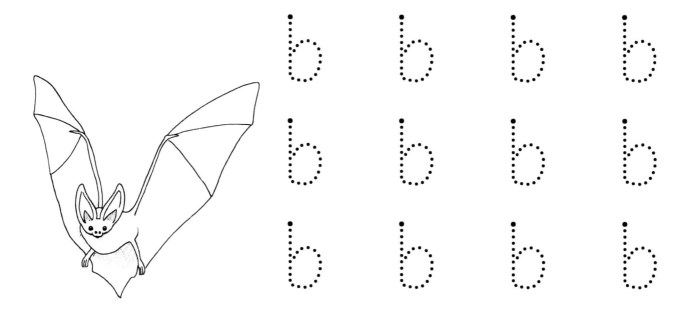

....

Write the over the dotted words. Then write the words by yourself.

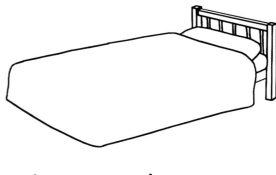

....

Activities from Jelly and Bean at Follifoot Farm

Name.......................... Date........................

Write over the dotted words. Then write them by yourself.

| **bag   bed   bad   bat** |

Say each word to a friend.

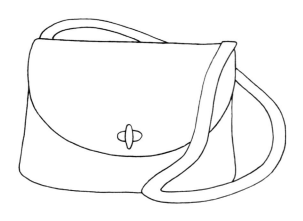 

 ....  ....

  ....

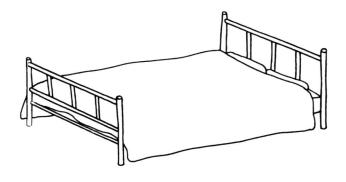

Activities from Jelly and Bean

Name..............................Date..............................

Write **a** in each word.

Draw a line from each word to the correct picture.

Name.............................Date...............................

Write e in each word.

Draw a line from each word to the correct picture.

Name............................Date............................

Write over the dotted letters. Then write the letters by yourself.

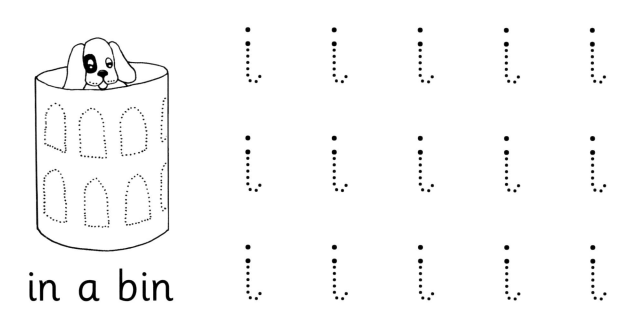

in a bin

....

Write the over the dotted words. Then write the words by yourself.

in a bin

....

Activities from Jelly and Bean

Name..Date...............................

Write over the dotted letters. Then write the letters by yourself.

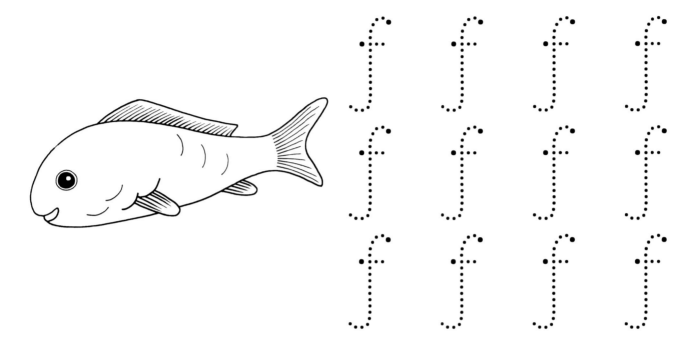

....

Write the over the dotted words. Then write the words by yourself.

....

Activities from Jelly and Bean

Name............................Date............................

Write over the dotted letters. Then write the letters by yourself.

l l l l l
l l l l l
l l l l l

....

l i l t l
i f i f t l
f t f l

....

Activities from Jelly and Bean

Name........................Date............................

Draw a line from each word to the correct picture.

Write the correct word under each picture.

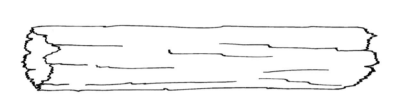　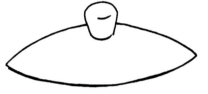

....　..........................

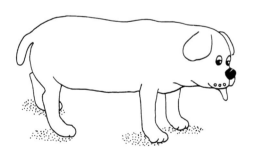　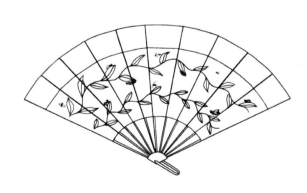

....　..........................

Activities from Jelly and Bean

Name......................................Date................................

Write **o** in each word.

Draw a line from each word to the correct picture.

Activities from Jelly and Bean

Name......................................Date......................................

Write over the dotted letters. Then write the letters by yourself.

m m m m m

m m m m m

....

m n r h n m

r h m r h n

m r n h m r

Activities from Jelly and Bean

Name.............................Date...............................

Write over the dotted letters. Then write the letters by yourself.

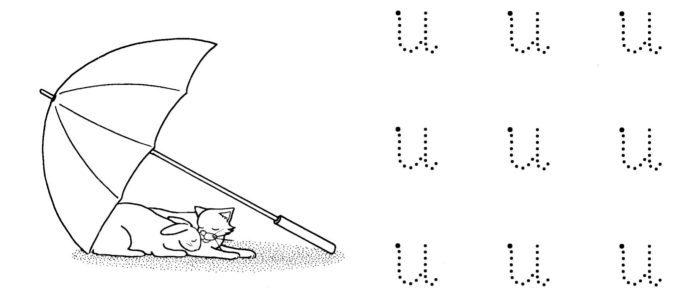

....

Write the over the dotted words. Then write the words by yourself.

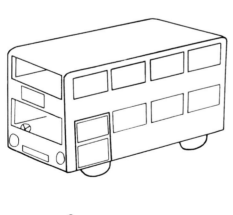 

....

Activities from Jelly and Bean

Name.............................Date...............................

Write the over the dotted words. Then write the words by yourself.

| **hug bun bud sun** |

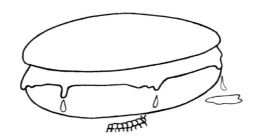

bun ....

hug ....

sun ....

bud ....

Activities from Jelly and Bean

27

Name.............................Date.............................

Write over the dotted letters. Then write the letters by yourself.

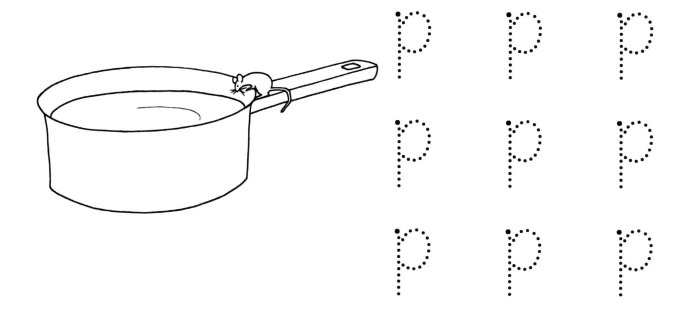

....

Write the over the dotted words. Then write the words by yourself.

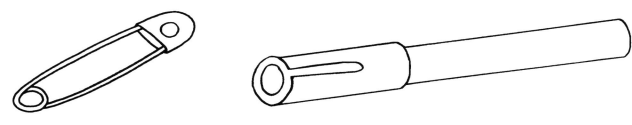

pin   pen

....

Activities from Jelly and Bean

Name.............................Date................................

Write **i** in each word.

Draw a line from each word to the correct picture.

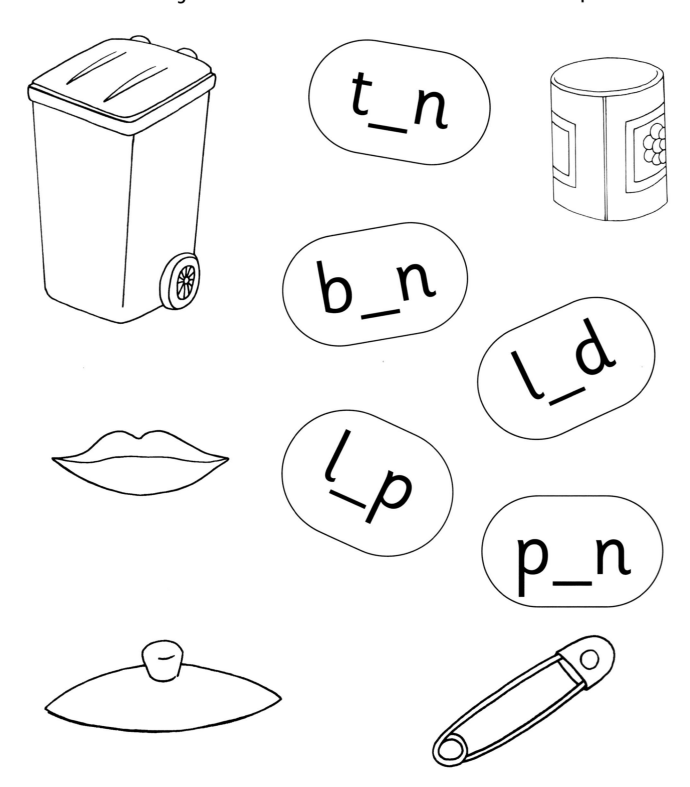

Activities from Jelly and Bean

29

Name.............................Date...............................

Write **u** in each word.

Draw a line from each word to the correct picture.

Activities from Jelly and Bean

Name............................Date................................

Write over the dotted letters. Then write the letters by yourself.

....

Write the over the dotted word. Then write the word by yourself.

kitten ....

Activities from Jelly and Bean

Name................................Date..................................

Write over the dotted letters. Then write the letters by yourself.

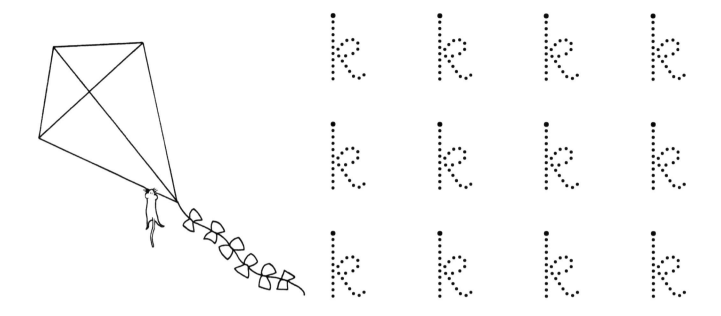

....

Write the over the dotted word. Then write the word by yourself.

kitten ....

Activities from Jelly and Bean

Name.............................Date......................

Write over the dotted letters. Write the words on the dotted line.

a fat dog

....

a mad man

....

a big hug

....

a red hen

Activities from Jelly and Bean

....

Name.............................Date.............................

Write over the dotted letters. Write the words on the dotted line.

the sun

....

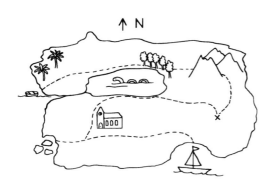

the map

....

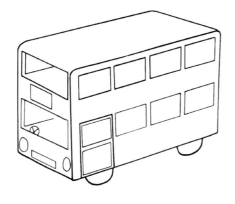

the bus

....

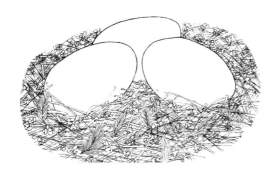

the eggs

....

Activities from Jelly and Bean

Name.................................Date...............................

Write over the dotted letters.   Write the words on the dotted line.

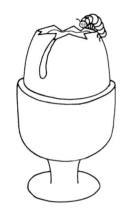

on the egg

....

on the pot

....

on the hat

....

on the bed

....

Activities from Jelly and Bean

Name..............................Date................................

Draw a line from each word to the correct picture.

Write the correct words under each picture.

on the pot

on the bed

on the mat

on the pan

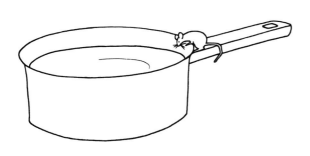

Activities from Jelly and Bean

Name.................................Date...............................

Write over the dotted letters.   Write the words on the dotted line.

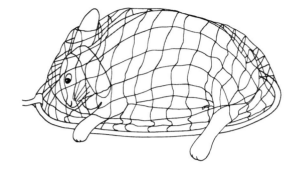

in the net

....

in the net

....

in the bag

....

in the tub

....

Activities from Jelly and Bean

Name.............................Date...............................

Draw a line from the each set of words to the correct picture.

in the bag

in the net

in the den

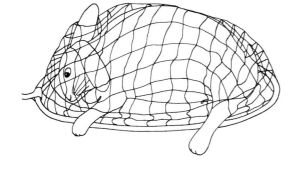

in the mud

in the tub

Activities from Jelly and Bean

Name.............................. Date..............................

Write over the dotted letters.   Write the words on the dotted line.

a bat and a cat

....

a dog and a frog

....

Activities from Jelly and Bean

Name............................Date..............................

Draw a line from the words to the correct picture.

| a hen and a rat | a cat and a bat |

| a frog and a dog | a pin and a tin |

Activities from Jelly and Bean

Name.............................. Date..............................

Write over the dotted sentences.   Write the sentence on the line.

   I am a rat.

....

   I am a hen.

....

I am a rabbit.

....

Activities from Jelly and Bean

Name..Date...........................

Write over the dotted sentences. Write the sentence on the line.

I can run.

....

I can hop.

....

I can dig.

....

I can sit.

....

Activities from Jelly and Bean

Name.............................Date...............................

Draw a line from each sentence to the correct picture.

Write each sentence below its picture.

| I am a dog. | I am a hen. |
| I am a bat. | I am a kitten. |

....

....

Activities from Jelly and Bean

Name............................Date................................

Draw a line from each sentence to the correct picture.

Write each sentence below its picture.

| I can run. | I can hop. |
| I can dig. | I can sit. |

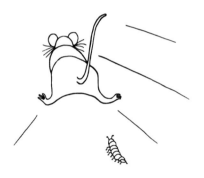

....

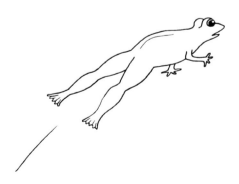

....

Activities from Jelly and Bean

Name............................Date............................

Draw a line from each sentence to the correct picture.

 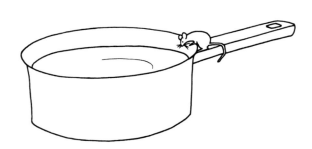

| I am on the pan. | I am in a net. |

| I am on a hat. | I am in the bin. |

 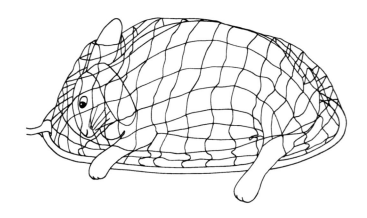

Activities from Jelly and Bean

Name.............................Date...............................

Write the correct word under each picture.

| bus cat dog fan hen
| mat pan rat sun |

....

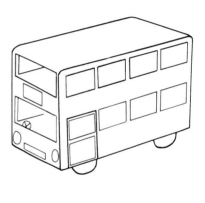

....

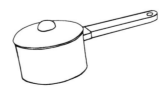

....

Activities from Jelly and Bean

46